KNOW ABOUT
ASTRONOMY

Know about Astronomy

Published by

MAPLE PRESS PRIVATE LIMITED
office: A-63, Sector 58, Noida 201301, U.P., India
phone: +91 120 455 3581, 455 3583
email: info@maplepress.co.in
website: www.maplepress.co.in

Reprinted in 2019

ISBN: 978-93-50335-65-9

Contents

Preface

Astronomy initially began about thousands of years ago as a descriptive science, tracking the motion of the Sun, Moon, Planets and Stars.

And the ancient people used their observations to keep track of time, plan agricultural planting, orient their cities, and to try to predict the future. Early astronomy was a mix of careful observation of the positions and motions of the heavenly bodies, religion, and astrology.

But with the changing age, astronomers were more concerned with studying and understanding the celestial bodies and their phenomena i.e., Why & How are these celestial bodies moving around in the space. Gradually as technology grew astronomers and space institutes started monitoring the universe closely and constantly trying to track the various actions and reactions happening in the space.

The term 'Astronomy' means the 'Laws of the Stars' and is therefore very appropriate. Understanding astronomical phenomena and their evolution requires extensive application of mathematics, physics, and chemistry, hence most astronomers call themselves astrophysicists.

This book takes you on a tour to the Universe and sums up facts about the entire solar System and its components.

CHAPTER 1
The Universe

The study of the Universe is not new to astronomy it is the oldest of all natural sciences. People have been trying to explain the formation and development of universe since many long years. Astronomers of early civilization performed methodical observations of the night sky and studied the movement of celestial bodies to determine celebrations and planting cycles. The ancient Greeks were the first to start developing astronomical theories about the design of the Universe. Previous observations of the moon had already led to the knowledge that the Earth was round.

The original Geocentric or Earth-Centred view of the Universe was formed when Plato gave his assertion that the sphere of the Earth is in perfect geometric shape.

Many earlier scientists believed that the heaven was a giant bowl covering the Earth, this new philosophy, expounded by Astronomer Eudoxus and Philosopher Aristotle in the 4th century B.C., said the sun, moon and planets hung on concentric spheres, all surrounding the

Earth. Although, this philosophy was helpful to ancient people in trying to sense the facts of an unknown Universe, however, this model did not help in proper tracking of the planets, moon and stars. Still, with few refinements, it remained the predominant scientific view of the Universe for another 600 years.

In the 2nd century, Claudius Ptolemaeus (Ptolemy), a Roman astronomer working in Egypt, added epicycles to the geocentric model. He said that the planets moved in perfect circles, attached to perfect spheres that all rotated around the Earth. While it was wrong, this theory could, at least, predict the paths of the planets fairly well. This view remained in use for another 1400 years.

In the 16th century, Nicolaus Copernicus, a Polish Astronomer, tired of the cumbersome and imprecise

nature of the Ptolemaic Model, began working on a theory of his own. He theorised that the Sun was stationary in the centre of the Universe and that the Earth and other planets revolved around it. The Copernicus Model of the Universe, while still incorrect, did three main things. It explained the prograde and retrograde motions of the planets. It took the Earth out of its spot as the centre of the universe. And, it expanded the size of the Universe. In a geocentric model, the size of the Universe is limited so that it can revolve once every twenty-four hours or else the stars would get slung off due to the centrifugal force. While it was a major step in the right direction, Copernicus' theories were still quite cumbersome and imprecise. His book, "On the Revolutions of the Heavenly Spheres", which was published in 1953 as he lay on his deathbed, was still a key element in the beginning of the Renaissance and the Age of Enlightenment.

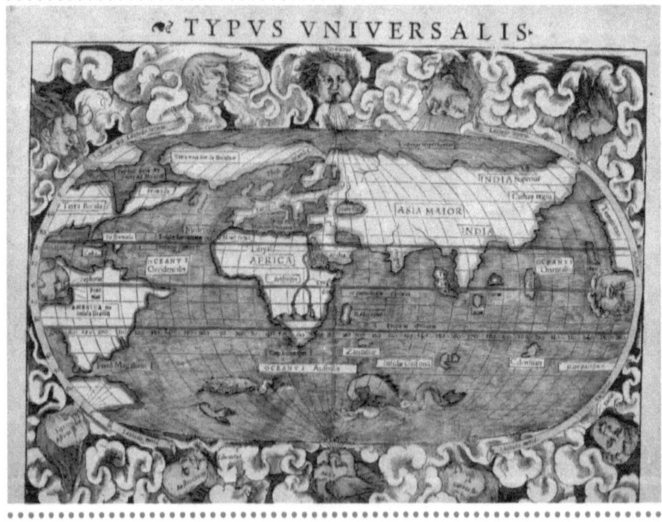

CHAPTER 2
The History

The early theories of the Universe and astronomy, while were very clever, all had the same problem. They all were based on incorrect assumptions, information and beliefs. To create an accurate model, one must first begin with accurate data.

The observations of Tycho Brahe and his assistant, Johannes Kepler was able to determine that the circle was not the correct goemetric form to explain planetary motions. As a mathematician, he knew that a circle is just a specialised ellipse. Utilising non-circular ellipses, he was able to calculate orbits, which correctly predicted planetary positions. He could not directly measure a planet's exact orbital size, but he was able to measure the ratio by using his equation and Brahe's observations. In the early 17th century, Galileo Galilei used surfaces of varying smoothness to slide blocks across to understand effects on body's motion. He found that rough tables made objects slow down at a faster rate than smooth ones. Extrapolating from these observations, he theorised that if a surface were completely smooth, objects would continue moving forever.

If you have studied physics, you will recognise this as the basis for the theory of inertia. Objects in motion tend to stay in motion in a straight line and objects at rest tend to stay at rest, unless acted upon by an external force.

Now they knew why the planets were moving, but they did not know why were in a circle? Why not keep

travelling in straight lines and fly off into deep space?

This was answered by Sir Isaac Newton when he published Philosophiae Naturalis Principia Mathematica. He theorised that the external force that kept the planets in orbit was the pull of gravity. According to Newton, the same force that causes an apple fall to the ground also explains why the moon continually 'falls' around the Earth. Meanwhile, the view of the Universe kept evolving. Kepler calculated his three laws of planetary motion, which gave a more accurate picture. Galileo's discovery of the moons of Jupiter with the newly invented telescope lent credence to the sun-centred model of the solar system. The Laws of Planetary Motion were a major building block in the foundation of modern astronomy.

CHAPTER 3
Milky Way Galaxy

The Universe is huge, larger than most of you can even imagine. Perhaps in a nod to the old belief of the Earth being the centre of the universe, the first unit of measurement is based on the distance of your home to the sun. The earth is 93 million miles from the sun, but it is much simpler to say that it is one Astronomical Unit (AU) from the sun. This measuring unit is best used to calculate the distance with our solar system. However, in order to evaluate the distance between of objects outside our solar system we needed a different measuring system.

Hence was created a unit of measure based on the distance that light travels in a year. This unit is called the "light years". A light year is 6 trillion miles (6,000,000,000 miles). The closest star to our solar system is actually a system of three stars called the Alpha Centauri System, consisting of Alpha Centauri, Rigil Kentaurus and Proxima Centauri, which is actually slightly closer than her sisters. Alpha Centauri is 4.3 light years from Earth. In order to measure larger distances, the parsec (Parallax Second) was invented. A parsec is approximately 3.258 light years. Along with the parsec, larger distances are measured in kiloparsecs (thousand parsecs) and mega parsecs (million parsecs).

Another way to denote very large numbers is called scientific notation. This system is based on the number ten and is written like this 1 x 101. This number equals 10. The one located to the right of the 10 indicates how many times 10 is used as a multiplier. In this case, once, so the number equals 10. Therefore, 1 x 102 would be the same as 1 x (10 x 10) or 100.

The Universe has gas

Stars are massive shining spheres of hot gas, the closest of which is the Sun. Those stars which you see with your naked eyes in the night sky all belong to the Milky Way

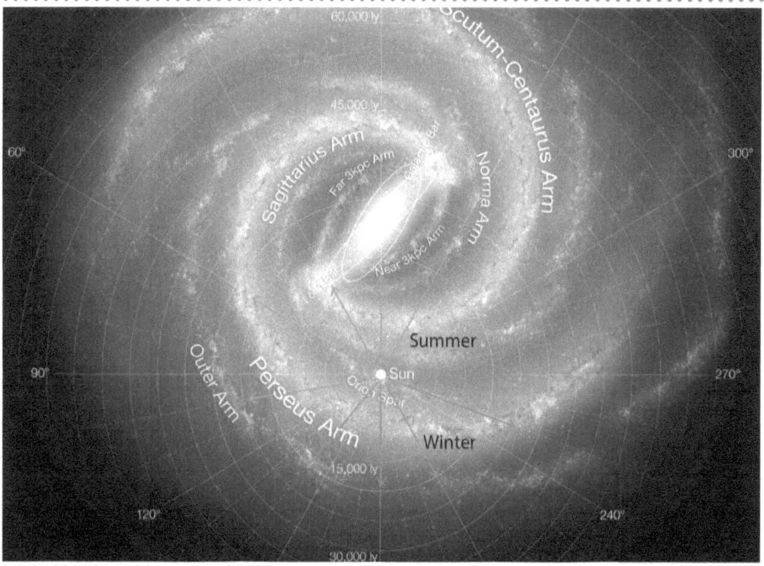

Galaxy, the huge system of stars that contains our solar system. There are around 5,000 stars which can be seen with the naked eye, though not all stars are visible at all times and places.

By taking the help of a small telescope, hundreds of thousands of stars can be seen. Larger-telescopes can show millions of galaxies, many of which may contain over 200 billion stars each. Today, scientists believe there are more than 1 x 1022 stars in the universe (10,000,00 0,000,000,000,000,000). Many of these stars are so large that if they took the Sun's place, they would engulf Earth, Mars, Jupiter and Saturn.

Stars come in a wide variety of colours, ranging from deep red, through orange and yellow to an intense white-blue. The colour of a star depends on its temperature. Cooler stars tend to be red, while the hottest ones are blue. Stars are divided into six brightness groups, which are called magnitudes. First magnitude is the brightest and sixth magnitude is the faintest. Each star's magnitude is 2.5 times brighter than the next lower star.

CHAPTER 4
Stars

Stars are made of hydrogen, smaller amounts of helium and trace amounts of other elements. Even the most abundant of the other elements present in stars (oxygen, carbon, neon and nitrogen) are only present in very small quantities.

Despite the wide spread use of phrases like 'the emptiness of space', space is definitely not empty. It is full of gasses and dust. This can even be seen as clouds of dust obscure the view of many stars. This matter can become compressed by any number of celestial events, including collisions and blast waves from exploding stars, causing lumps of matter to form.

If the gravity of these lumps of matter is strong enough, they can pull in other matter for fuels and as they continue to compress, their internal temperatures are raised to such a point that the hydrogen ignites in thermonuclear fusion. While the gravity continues pulling, trying to collapse the star into the smallest possible size, the fusion stabilises it, preventing further contraction. Thus, a great struggle

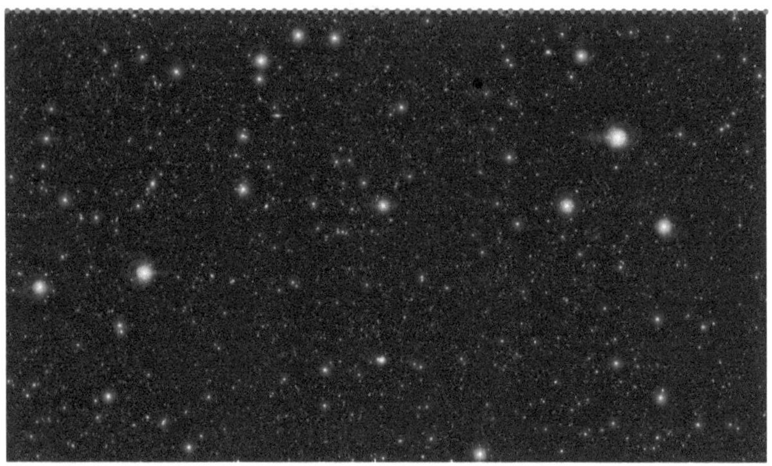

ensues for the life of the star, as each force continues to push or pull.

Many of these stars have their own systems of planets, moons, asteroids, and comets. Thermonuclear fusion is the process in which a star produces its light, heat, and energy . This happens when a star finds a way to combine four hydrogen atoms to make a helium atom. This fusion releases certain amount of energy which is converted into light and heat.

Eventually, most of the fuel, hydrogen, is exhausted. As the fuel begins to reduce, the strength of the thermonuclear fusion reaction declines. Soon gravity will win and the star will collapse under its own weight. At that time, it becomes what is known as a white dwarf. As the fuel further depletes and reaction stops all together, it will collapse further, into a black dwarf. This process can take billions and billions of years to complete.

Towards the end of the twentieth century, astronomers began to discover planets orbiting other stars. Because planets are so much smaller and fainter than stars, they are difficult to detect and impossible to see, so how do scientists find them? They measure tiny wobbles in a star's motion caused by the gravitational pull of the planets. Although, no Earth-like planets have been discovered yet, scientists are hopeful.

Just like when you travel, you need a road map to find your path, when you search the skies, you need a sky map to lead you to the stars. There are many very good maps for sale at hobby shops that specialise in astronomy, but before spending money, check out the free maps you can create. These will work just fine for your first forays into the stars.

CHAPTER 5
The Look and Patterns of the Stars

In order to have the best views of the sky, you should try to find a nice size field, preferably with as little light around as possible to minimise the light pollution. Light pollution is any light around you, which prevents your eyes from adjusting to die dark, thereby making stargazing more difficult. Your back yard may work just fine.

If you are located south of the equator, it is possible you will want a different landmark. Probably the most easily recognisable constellation, which can be seen from the southern hemisphere, is the Southern Cross. Once you locate this constellation, use it to orient yourself on the sky map. Do not expect to see everything at once, it is a very large universe. Remember that the Earth is constantly moving, so allow for that movement as you look at the map.

Here is a listing of the 25 brightest stars. Remember that not all of these stars will be visible from where you are or at the time, you are looking.

Common Name	Distance (light years)	Apparent Magnitude	Absolute Magnitude
Sun	-	-26.72	4.8
Sirius	8.6	-1.46	1.4
Canopus	74	-0.72	-2.5
Rigil Kentaurus	4.3	-0.27	4.4
Arcturus	34	-0.04	0.2
Vega	25	0.03	0.6
Capella	41	0.08	0.4
Rigel	~1400	0.12	-8.1
Procyon	11.4	0.38	2.6
Achernar	69	0.46	-1.3
Betelgeuse	~1400	0.50 (var.)	-7.2
Hadar	320	0.61 (var.)	-4.4

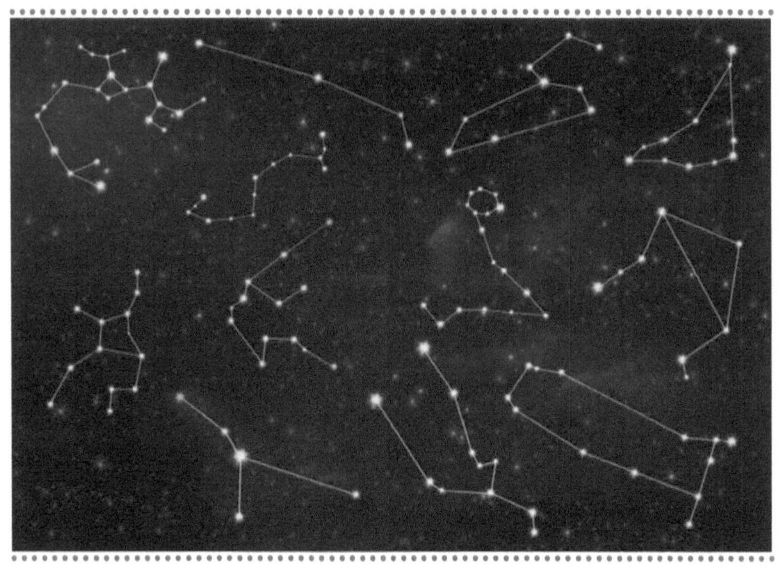

Acrux	510	0.76	-4.6
Altair	16	0.77	2.3
Aldebaran	60	0.85 (var.)	-0.3
Antares	~520	0.96 (var.)	-5.2
Spica	220	0.98 (var.)	-3.2
Pollux	40	1.14	0.7
Fomalhaut	22	1.16	2.0
Becrux	460	1.25 (var.)	-4.7
Deneb	1500	1.25	-7.2
Regulus	69	1.35	-0.3
Adhara	570	1.50	-4.8
Castor	49	1.57	0.5
Gacrux	120	1.63 (var.)	-1.2
Shaula	330	1.63 (var.)	-3.5

The Patterns

In ancient days, people looked at the sky and the stars, wondered about what they saw. This started long before the birth of astronomy.

Besides stargazing, they played a version of the modern kids game, connect the dots and named patterns of stars after what they reminded them of. Then they created stories about these constellations.

Most of the constellations that are discussed today arc over 2000 years old. As a matter of fact, the constellations Ursa Major and Ursa Minor, the Big Bear and the Little Bear, have been constellations since the Ice Ages. Most names, however, come from ancient Greece.

Although, the Greek versions are mostly what are used today to describe the constellations, many other cultures throughout the world created their own patterns and stories for the stars.

Although, most people can recognise the Big Dipper, it is not really a constellation. It is what is known as an asterism or a group of stars. It is actually part of a larger constellation called Ursa Major. Likewise, the Little Dipper is a part of Ursa Minor. On the other hand, the landmark' for the south, the Southern Cross is an actual constellation called Crux.

CHAPTER 6
The Solar System

It consists of a star orbited by planets or smaller rocky bodies and the gravitational pull of the star holds the system together. Our solar system consists of the sun, which is a star called Sol, nine planets including the Earth, alongwith the satellites of those planets, a number of asteroids, comets and other smaller objects.

The Sun

While some stars in our galaxy are nearly as old as the universe, about 15 billion years, the sun is a second-generation star. It is only 4.6 billion years old. Some of its material came from former stars.

Sol

The Sun is a normal G2 star, one of more than 100 billion stars in our galaxy.

Diameter.1,390,000km

Mass: 1.989^{e30}kg

Temp: 5800K (surface) 15,600,000 K (core)

The Sun is by far the largest object in the solar system. It contains more than 99.8% of the total mass of the Solar System.

The Sun is personified in many mythologies: the Greeks called it Helios and the Romans called it Sol. The Sun is, at present, about 70 % hydrogen and 28 % helium by mass, everything else ('metals') amounts to less than 2%. 'This changes slowly over time as the Sun converts hydrogen to helium in its core.

The outer layers of the Sun exhibit differential rotation: at the equator, the surface rotates once every 25.4 days. Near the poles, it is as much as 36 days.

Conditions at the Sun's core (approximately the inner 25 % of its radius) are extreme. The temperature is 15.6 million Kelvin and the pressure is 250 billion atmospheres. At the centre of the core, the Sun's density is more than 150 times that of water.

The Sun's energy output (3.86e33 ergs/second or 386 billion billion megawatts) is produced by nuclear fusion reactions. Each second about 700,000,000 tons of hydrogen are converted to about 695,000,000 tons of helium and 5,000,000 tons (=3.86e33 ergs) of energy in the form of gamma rays.

The surface of the Sun, called the photosphere, is at a temperature of about 5800 K. Sunspots are 'cool' regions, only 3800 K.

A small region known as the chromosphere lies above the photosphere. The highly rarefied region above the chromosphere, called the corona, extends millions of kilometres into space but is visible only during eclipses. Temperatures in the corona are over 1,000,000 K. The Sun's magnetic field is very strong and very complicated. Its magnetosphere(also known as the heliosphere) extends well beyond Pluto.

The Sun also emits a low-density stream of charged particles (mostly electrons and protons) known as the solar wind, which propagates throughout the solar system at about 450 km/sec

CHAPTER 7
Some Findings

Recent data from a study shows that during the minimum of the solar cycle the solar wind emanating from the Polar Regions flow at nearly double the rate, 750 kilometres per second that it does at lower latitudes. The composition of the solar wind also appears to differ in the Polar Regions. During the solar maximum, however, the solar wind moves at an intermediate speed.

Further study of the solar wind will be done by Wind, ACE and SOHO spacecraft from the dynamically stable vantage point directly between the Earth and the Sun about 1.6 million km from Earth. The solar wind has large effects on the tails of comets and even has measurable effects on the trajectories of spacecraft.

Spectacular loops and prominences are often visible on the Sun's limb.

The Sun's output is not entirely constant, nor is the amount of sunspot activity. There was a period of very low sunspot activity in the latter half of the 17th century called the Maunder Minimum. It coincides with an abnormally

cold period in northern Europe sometimes known as the 'little Ice Age'. Since the formation of the solar system, the Sun's output has increased by about 40%.

The Sun is about 4.5 billion years old. Since its birth, it has used up about half of the hydrogen in its core. It will continue- to radiate 'peacefully' for another 5 billion years or so (although its luminosity will approximately double in that time). But eventually it will run out of hydrogen fuel. It will then be forced into radical changes, which, though commonplace by stellar standards, will result in the total destruction of the Earth (and probably the creation of a planetary nebula).

The Sun's satellites

There are nine planets and a large number of smaller objects orbiting the Sun.

Planet	Distance (000km)	Radius (km)	Mass (kg)
Mercury	57,910	2,439	3.30e23
Venus	108,200	6,052	4.87e24
Earth	149,600	6,378	5.98e24
Mars	227,940	3,397	6.42e24
Jupiter	778,330	71,492	1.90e27
Saturn	1,426,940	60,268	5.69e26
Uranus	2,870,990	25,559	8.69e25
Neptune	4,497,070	24,764	1.02e26
Pluto	5,913,520	11,60	1.31e22

CHAPTER 8
Mercury

Mercury is the closest planet to the Sun and the eighth largest. Mercury is smaller in diameter than the satellite moons Ganymede and Titan but more massive.

Orbit. 57,910,000 km (0.38 AU) from Sun

Diameter. 4,880 km

Mass: 3.30e23 kg

Mercury has been known since at least the time of the Sumerians (3rd millennium B.C.). It was given two names by the Greeks: 'Apollo' for its apparition as a morning star and 'Hermes' as an evening star. Greek astronomers knew, however that the two names referred to the same body. Heraclitus even believed that Mercury and Venus orbit the Sun, not the Earth. Mercury has been visited by two spacecrafts, Mariner10 and MESSENGER. Mariner10 flew by three times in 1974 and 1975. However only 45% of the surface could be mapped. MESSENGER was launched by NASA in 2004 and has been in orbit Mercury since 2011. Its first flyby in Jan 2008 provided new high quality images of some of the terrain not seen by Mariner 10. Since then Messenger has taken over 250,000 photographs coving the entire planet. Mercury's orbit is highly eccentric, at perihelion, it is only 46 million kms from the Sun but at aphelion, it is 70 million kms. The perihelion of its orbit processes around the Sun at a very slow rate.

Until 1962, it was thought that Mercury's 'day' was the same length as its 'year' so as to keep that same face to the Sun much as the Moon does to the Earth. But this was shown to be false in 1965. It is now known that Mercury rotates three times in two of its years. Mercury is the only body in the solar system known to have an orbital/ rotational resonance with a ratio other than 1:1.

This fact and the high eccentricity of Mercury's orbit would produce very strange effects for an observer on

Mercury's surface. At some longitudes, the observer would see the Sun rise and then gradually increases in apparent size as it slowly moved towards the zenith. Mercury's surface is heavily cratered and very cold. Mercury is the second densest major body in the solar system and it's dense iron core is relatively larger than Earth's, probably comprises the majority of the planet. Mercury therefore has only a relatively thin silicate mantle and crust.

Mercury's interior is dominated by a large iron core whose radius is 1800 to 1900 km. The silicate outer shell (analogous to Earth's mantle and crust) is only 500 to 600 km thick. At least some of the core is probably molten. Measurements from the Messenger spacecraft show Mercury's magnetic field is approximately three times stronger in the northern hemisphere than the southern hemisphere

A reanalysis of the Mariner data provides four preliminary evidence of Mercury. First, amazingly, radar observations of Mercury's north pole show evidence of water ice in the protected shadows of some craters. Second, Mercury has a small magnetic field whose strength is about 1% of Earth's. Third, Mercury has no known satellites. Fourth, Mercury is often visible with binoculars or even the unaided eye, but it is always very near the Sun and difficult to see in the twilight sky.

CHAPTER 9
Venus

Venus is the second planet from the Sun and the sixth largest. Venus' orbit is the most nearly circular of that of any planet, with an eccentricity of less than 1%.

Orbit. 108,200,000 km (0.72 A(J) from Sun

Diameter. 12,103.6km

Mass. 4.869e24 kg

Venus (Greek: Aphrodite, Babylonian: Ishtar) is the Goddess of love and beauty. It is the brightest object in the sky except for the Sun and the Moon. Like Mercury, it was popularly thought to be two separate bodies: Eosphorus as the 'morning star' and Hesperus as the 'evening star', but the Greek astronomers knew better.

The first spacecraft to visit Venus was Mariner 2 in 1962. It was subsequently visited by many others (more than 20 in all so far), including Pioneer Venus and the Soviet Venera 7 the first spacecraft to land on another planet and Venera 9, which returned the first photographs of the surface.

Venus' rotation is somewhat unusual in that it is both very slow (243 Earth days per Venus day, slightly longer than Venus' year) and retrograde.

Venus is sometimes regarded as Earth's sister planet. In some ways, they are very similar

- Venus is only slightly smaller than Earth (95% of Earth's diameter, 80% of Earth's mass).

- Both have few craters indicating relatively young surfaces.

- Their densities and chemical compositions are similar.

The pressure of Venus' atmosphere at the surface is 90 atmospheres (about the same as the pressure at a depth of 1 km in Earth's oceans). It is composed mostly of carbon dioxide. This dense atmosphere produces a run-away greenhouse effect that raises Venus' surface temperature

by about 400 degrees to over 740 K. Venus' surface is actually hotter than Mercury's despite being nearly twice as far from the Sun. Venus probably once had large amounts of water like Earth but it all boiled away. Venus is now quite dry.

Facts and data show that much of the surface of Venus is covered by lava flows. Recently announced findings indicate that Venus is still volcanically active, but only in a few hot spots.

The oldest terrains on Venus seem to be about 800 million years old. Extensive volcanism at that time wiped out the earlier surface including any large craters from early in Venus' history.

The interior of Venus is probably very similar to that of Earth: an iron core about 3000 km in radius, a molten rocky mantle comprising the majority of the planet.

- Venus has no magnetic field, perhaps because of its slow rotation.

- Venus has no satellites and thereby hangs a tale.

- Venus is usually visible with the unaided eye. Sometimes (inaccurately) referred to as the 'morning star' or the 'evening star', it is by far the brightest 'star' in the sky.

CHAPTER 10
Earth

Earth is the third planet from the Sun and the fifth largest:

Orbit 149,600,000 km (1.00 AU) from Sun

Diameter.12,756.3 km *Mass*: 5.972^{tl24} kg

Earth is the only planet whose English name does not derive from Greek/Roman mythology. The name derives from Old English and Germanic. In Roman Mythology,

the Goddess of the Earth was Tellus - the fertile soil (Greek:, terra mater - Mother Earth). It was not until the time of Copernicus (the sixteenth century) that it was understood that the Earth is just another planet.

Earth, of course, can be studied without the aid of spacecraft. Pictures of the planet taken from space are of considerable importance. For example, they are an enormous help in weather prediction and especially in tracking and predicting hurricanes.

The Earth is divided into several layers, which have distinct chemical and seismic properties (depths in km):

0-40	Crust
40-400	Upper mantle
400- 650	Transition region
650-2700	Lower mantle
2700-2890	D" layer
2890-5150	Outer core
5150-6378	Inner core

The Earth's inner core and crust are solid. The outer core and mantle layers are plastic or semi-fluid. The various layers are separated by discontinuities, which are evident in seismic data.

The best known of these is the Mohorovicic discontinuity between the crust and upper mantle.

Most of the mass of the Earth is in the mantle, most of the rest in the core. The part that is inhabited is a tiny fraction of the whole (values below x10^24 kilograms):

Atmosphere   =   0.0000051

Oceans   =   0.0014

Crust   =   0.026

Mantle   =   4.043

Outer core   =   1.835

Inner core   =   0.09675

The core is probably composed mostly of iron (or nickel/iron). Temperatures at the centre of the core may be as high as 7500 K, hotter than the surface of the Sun. The lower mantle is probably mostly silicon, magnesium and oxygen with some iron, calcium and aluminium. The upper mantle is mostly olivene and pyroxene (iron/magnesium silicates), calcium and aluminium. The crust is primarily quartz (silicon dioxide) and other silicates like feldspar.

Taken as a whole, the Earth's chemical composition (by mass) is:

34.6% Iron

29.5% Oxygen

15.2% Silicon

12.7% Magnesium

2.4% Nickel

1.9% Sulphur

0.05% Titanium

The Earth is the densest major body in the solar system.

The other terrestrial planets probably have similar structures and compositions with some differences:

The Moon has at most a small core.

- Mercury has an extra large core (relative to its diameter).

- The mantles of Mars and the Moon are much thicker.

- The Moon and Mercury may not have chemically distinct crusts. Earth may be the only one with distinct inner and outer cores.

Note, however that the knowledge of planetary interiors is mostly theoretical even for the Earth.

CHAPTER 11
The Plates

The Earth's crust is divided into several separate solid plates, which float around independently on top of the hot mantle below. The theory that describes this is known as plate tectonics. It is characterised by two major processes: spreading and subduction. Spreading occurs when two plates move away from each other and new crust is created by upwelling magma from below. Subduction occurs

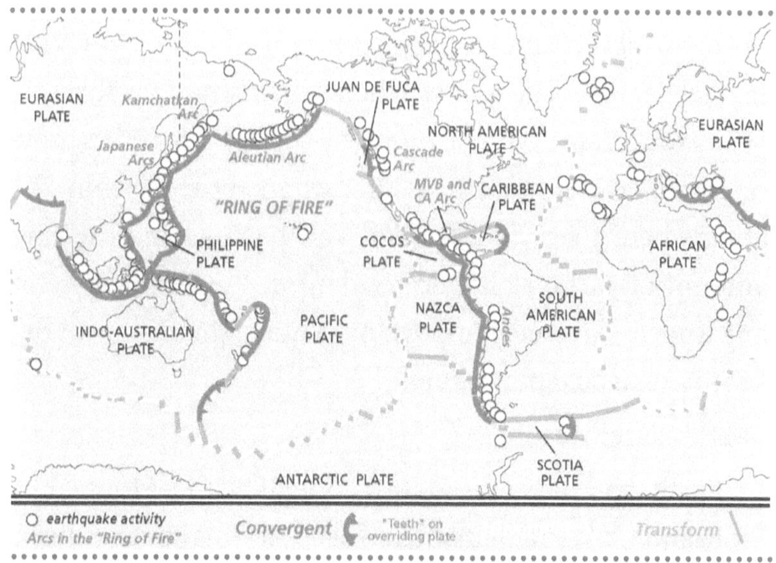

when two plates collide and the edge of one dives beneath the other and ends up being destroyed in the mantle. There are eight major plates namely, North American Plate, South American Plate, Antarctic Plate, Eurasian Plate, African Plate, Indian-Australian Plate, Nazca Plate and Pacific Plate.

71 % of the Earth's surface is covered with water. Earth is the only planet on which water can exist in liquid form on the surface. Liquid water is, of course, essential for life but Liquid water is also responsible for most of the erosion and weathering of the Earth's continents, a process unique in the solar system today. The heat capacity of the oceans is also very important in keeping the Earth's temperature relatively stable.

The Earth's atmosphere is 77 % nitrogen, 21% oxygen, with traces of argon, carbon dioxide and water. There was probably a very much larger amount of carbon dioxide in the Earth's atmosphere when Earth was first formed. However, Plate tectonics and biological processes now maintain a continual flow of carbon dioxide from the atmosphere to various "sinks" and back again. The tiny amount of carbon dioxide resident in the atmosphere at any time is extremely important to the maintenance of the Earth's surface temperature.

Earth's Satellite

Earth has only one natural satellite, the Moon. But thousands of small artificial satellites have also been placed in orbit around the Earth.

Asteroids 3753 Cruithne and 2002 AA29 have complicated orbital relationships with the Earth. They are not really Moons, the term 'Companion' is being used. It is somewhat similar to the situation with Saturn's moons Janus and Epimetheus.

Satellite	Distance (000km)	Radius (km)	Muss (kg)
Moon	384	173	7.35e22

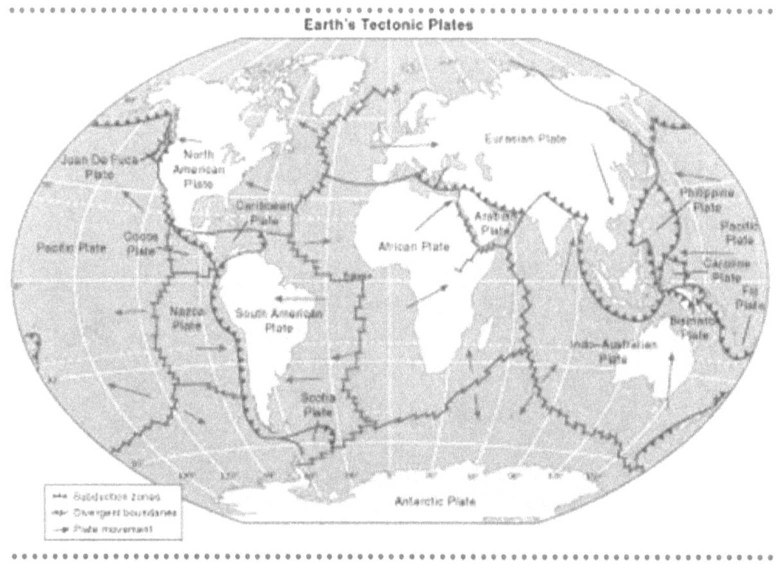

CHAPTER 12
Mars

Mars is the fourth planet from the Sun and the seventh largest.

Orbit. 227,940,000 km (1.52 AU) from Sun

Diameter. 6,794 Km

Mass. 6.4219$^{e23'}$ kg

Mars (Greek: Ares) is the God of War. The planet probably got this name due to its red colour referred to

as the Red Planet. The name of the month March derives from Mars.

The first spacecraft to visit Mars was Mariner 4 in 1965. Several others followed including Mars 2, the first spacecraft to land on Mars and the two Viking landers in 1976. Ending a long 20 year hiatus, Mars Pathfinder landed successfully on Mars on July 4,1997. In 2004 the Mars Expedition Rovers "Spirit" and "Opportunity" landed on Mars sending back geologic data and many pictures; they are still operating after more than three years on Mars. In 2008, Phoenix landed in the northern plains to search for water. The three Mars orbiters, Mars Reconnaissance Orbiter, Mars Odyssey, and Mars Express are also currently in operation.

Mars' orbit is significantly elliptical. One result of this is a temperature variation of about 30 °C at the sub-solar point between aphelion and perihelion. Though, Mars is much smaller than Earth, its surface area is about the same as the land surface area of Earth.

Mars has a very thin atmosphere composed mostly of the tiny amount of remaining carbon dioxide (95.3%) plus nitrogen (2.7%), argon (1.6%) and traces of oxygen (0.15%) and water (0.03%). The average pressure on the surface of Mars is only about 7 millibars (less than 1% of Earth's).

Mars has permanent ice caps at both poles composed of water ice and solid carbon dioxide ('dry ice'). The ice caps exhibit a layered structure with alternating layers of ice with varying concentrations of dark dust. The seasonal changes in the extent of the polar caps changes the global atmospheric pressure by about 25%.

Recent observations with the Hubble Space Telescope have revealed that the conditions during the Viking missions may not have been typical. Mars' atmosphere now seems to be both colder and dryer than measured by the Viking landers.

The Viking landers performed experiments to determine the existence of life on Mars. The results were somewhat ambiguous but most scientists now believe that they show no evidence for life on Mars Optimists point out that only two tiny samples were measured and not from the most favourable locations. More experiments will be done by future missions to Mars.

A small number of meteorites are believed to have originated on Mars. When it is in the night time sky, Mars is easily visible with the unaided eye. Its apparent brightness varies greatly according to its relative position to the Earth.

Mars' Satellites

Mars has two tiny satellites, which orbit very close to the surface:

Satellite	Distance (000 km)	Radius (km)	Mass (kg)
Phobos	9	11	1.08el6
Deimos	23	6	1.80el5

CHAPTER 13
Jupiter

Jupiter is the fifth planet from the Sun and by far the largest. Jupiter is more than twice as massive as all the other planets combined (318 times that of Earth).

Orbit: 778,330,000 km (5.20 AU) from Sun

Diameter: 142,984 km (equatorial)

Mass: 1.900e27kg

Jupiter (also known as Jove, Greek Zeus) was the King of the Gods, the ruler of Olympus and the patron of the Roman state. Zeus was the son of Cronus (Saturn).

Jupiter is the fourth brightest object in the sky (after the Sun, the Moon and Venus). It has been known since prehistoric times. Galileo's discovery, in 1610, of Jupiter's four large moons Io, Europa, Ganymede and Callisto (now known as the Galilean moons) was the first discovery of a centre of motion not apparently centred on the Earth.

Jupiter was first visited by Pioneer 10 in 1973 and later by Pioneer 11, Voyager 1, Voyager 2 and Ulysses. The spacecraft Galileo orbited Jupiter for eight years.

Jupiter is about 90 % hydrogen and 10 % helium (by numbers of atoms, 75/25 % by mass) with traces of methane, water, ammonia and rock. Jupiter probably has a core of rocky material amounting to something like 10 to 15 Earth masses. Above the core lies the main bulk of the planet in the form of liquid metallic hydrogen. This exotic form of the most common of elements is possible only at pressures exceeding 4 million bars, The outermost layer is composed primarily of ordinary molecular hydrogen and helium which is liquid in the interior and gaseous further out.

The Great Red Spot has been seen by Earthly observers for more than 300 years. The GRS is an oval about 12,000 by 25,000 km, big enough to hold two Earths.. Other smaller but similar spots have been known for decades.

Jupiter radiates more energy into space than it receives from the Sun. The interior of Jupiter is hot: the core is probably about 20,000K. Jupiter has a huge magnetic field, much stronger than Earth's.

The Galileo atmospheric probe discovered a new intense radiation belt between Jupiter's ring and the uppermost atmospheric layers. This new belt is approximately 10 times as strong as Earth's Van Alien radiation belts.

Jupiter's Satellites

Jupiter has 67 known satellites the four large Galilean moons, plus many more small ones some of them not yet named. Few of the named satellites are listed below:

Satellite	Distance (000 km)	Radius (km)	Mass (kg)
Metis	128	20	9.56e16
Adrastea	129	10	1.91e16
Amalthea	181	98	7.17e18
Thebe	999	50	7.77e17
Io	422	1815	8.94e22
Europa	671	1569	4.80e22
Ganymede	1070	2631	1.48e21
Callisto	1883	2400	1.08e23
Leda	11094	8	5.68e15
Himalia	11480	93	9.56e18
Lysithea	11720	18	7.77e18

Elara	11737	387	7.77 e17
Ananke	21200	15	3.82e16
Carme	22600	20	9.56e16
Pasiphae	23500	25	1.91e17
Sinope	23700	18	7.77e16

Values for the smaller moons are approximate. Jupiter's Rings

Jupiter's Rings

Ring	Distance (km)	Width (km)	Mass (kg)
Halo	100000	22800	?
Main	122800	6400	1e13
Gossamer	129200	214200	?

(distance is from Jupiter's centre to the ring's inner edge)

CHAPTER 14
Saturn

Saturn is the sixth planet from the Sun and the second largest.

Orbit 1,429,400,000 km (9.54 AU) from Sun

Diameter. 120,536 km (equatorial)

Mass: 5.68e26 kg

In Roman mythology, Saturn is the God of agriculture. The associated Greek God, Cronus, was the son of Uranus and Gaia and the father of Zeus (Jupiter). Saturn is the

root of the English word 'Saturday'. Galileo was the first to observe it with a telescope in 1610. Saturn was first visited by Pioneer 11 in 1979 and later by Voyager 1 and Voyager 2. In 2004 Cassini orbited Saturn for about 4 years.

Saturn is visibly flattened (oblate) when viewed through a small telescope. Its equatorial and polar diameters vary by almost 10 % (120,536 km vs. 108,728 km). Saturn is the least dense of the planets, its specific gravity (0.7) is less than that of water.

Saturn contains about 75 % hydrogen and 25 % helium with traces of water, methane, ammonia and rock. Saturn's interior is similar to Jupiter's consisting of a rocky core, liquid metallic hydrogen layer and a molecular hydrogen layer. Traces of various ices are also present. Saturn's interior is hot (12000 K at the core) and Saturn radiates more energy into space than it receives from the Sun.

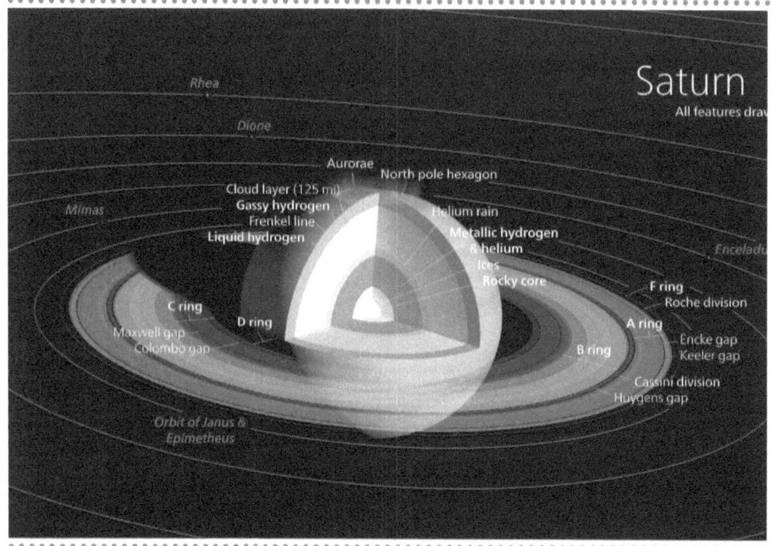

Saturn's rings are extraordinarily thin: though they are 250,000 km or more in diameter, they are less than one kilometre thick. The ring particles seem to be composed primarily of water ice, but they may also include rocky particles with icy coatings.

Saturn's outermost ring, the F-ring, is a complex structure made up of several smaller rings along which 'knots' are visible. When it is in the night time sky, Saturn is easily visible to the unaided eye. Though it is not nearly as bright as Jupiter, it is easy to identify as a planet because it doesn't "twinkle" like the stars do. The rings and the larger satellites are visible with a small astronomical telescope.

Saturn has 62 named satellites (as of 2010). There are 9 more that have been discovered but as yet not named.

The three pairs of satellites Mimas-Tethys, Enceladus-Dione and Titan-Hyperion interact gravitationally in such a way as to maintain stable relationships between their orbits:

List of major moons are:

Satellite	Distance (000km)	Width (km)	Mass (kg)
Pan	134	10	?
Atlas	138	14	?
Prometheus	139	46	2.70e17
Pandora	142	46	2.20e17
Epimetheus	151	57	5.60e17

Janus	151	89	2.01e18
Mimas	186	196	3.80e19
Enccladus	238	260	8.40e19
Tcthvs	295	530	7.55e20
Telcsto	295	15	?
Calypso	295	13	?
Dione	377	560	1.05e21
Helene	377	16	?
Rhea	527	765	?
Titan	1222	2575	1.35e23
Hyperion	1481	143	1.77e19
Iepetus	3561	730	1.88e21
Phoebe	12952	110	4.00e18

Saturn's Ring

Name	Radius inner	Radius approx. outer	width
D-Ring	67,000	74,500	7,500
Guerin Division			
C-Ring	74,500	92,000	17,500
Maxwell			
Division	87,500	88,000	500
B-Ring	92,000	117,500	25,500
Gassini			
Division	115,800	120,600	4,800

Huygens Gap	117,680	(n/a)	285-440
A-Ring	122,200	136,800	14,600
Encke Minima	126,430	129,940	3,500
Encke Division	133,580		325
F-Ring	140,210	30-500	
G-Ring	165,800	173,800	8,000
E-Ring	180,000	480,000 00,000	

This categorisation is actually somewhat misleading as the density of particles varies in a complex way not indicated by a division into neat regions: there are variations within the rings, the gaps are not entirely empty. The rings are not perfectly circular.

CHAPTER 15
Uranus

Uranus is the seventh planet from the Sun and the third largest (by diameter). Uranus is larger in diameter but smaller in mass than Neptune.

Orbit. 2,870,990,000 km (19.218 AU) from Sun

Diameter: 51,118 km (equatorial)

Mass: 8.683e25kg

Uranus is the ancient Greek deity of the Heavens, the earliest supreme god. Uranus was the son and mate of Gain the father of Cronus (Satyrn) and of the Cyclopes and Titans ('Predecessors of the Olympian gods).

Uranus was discovered by William Herschel while searching the sky with his telescope on March 13, 1781. It had actually been seen many times before but ignored as simple another star (the earliest recorded sighting was in 1690 when John Flamsted catalogued it as 34 Tauri). Herschel named it 'the Georgium Sidus' (the Georgian Planet) in honour of his patron, the infamous (to Americans) King George III of England. Others called it 'Herschel'. The name 'Uranus' was first proposed by Bode in 1850.

Uranus has been visited by only one spacecraft, Voyager 2 on January 24, 1986.

Uranus is composed primarily of rock and various ices, with only about 15 % hydrogen and a little helium (in contrast to Jupiter and Saturn which are mostly hydrogen). Uranus' atmosphere is about 83 % hydrogen, 15 % helium and 2 % methane.

Uranus is sometimes just barely visible with the unaided eye on a very clear night. It is fairly easy to spot with binoculars. A small astronomical telescope will show a small disk. Like the other gas planets, Uranus has bands of clouds that blow around rapidly. But they are extremely faint, visible only with radical image enhancement of the Voyager 2 pictures.

Uranus' blue color is the result of absorption of red light by methane in the upper atmosphere.

Uranus' Satellites

Uranus has 27 named moons and six unnamed ones.

Unlike classical mythology, Uranus' moons take their names from the writings of Shakespeare and Pope. Most have nearly circular orbits in the plane of Uranus' equator (and hence at a large angle to the plane of the ecliptic), the outer 4 are much more elliptical.

Satellite	Distance (000 km)	Radius (km)	Mass (kg)
Cordelia	50	13	?
Ophelia	54	16	?
Bianca	59	22	?
Cressida	62	33	?
Desdemona	63	29	?
Juliet	64	42	?
Portia	66	55	?
Rosalind	70	27	?
2003U2	75	6	?
Belinda	75	34	?
1986U10	76	40	?
Puck	86	77	?
2003U1	98	8	?
Miranda	130	236	6.30^{e19}

Ariel	191	579	1.27^{e21}
Umbriel	266	585	1.27^{e21}
Titania	436	789	3.49^{e21}
Obcron	583	761	3.03^{e21}
2001U 3	4281	6	?
Caliban	7169	40	?
Stephano	7948	15	?
Trinculo	8578	5	?
Sycorax	12213	80	?
2003U3	14689	6	?

Prospero	16568	20	?
Setebos	17681	20	?
2002U2	21000	6	

Uranus' Rings

Ring	Distance (km)	Width (km)
1986U2R	38000	2,500
6	41840	1-3
5	42230	2-3
4	42580	2-3
Alpha	44720	7-12
Beta	45670	7-12
Eta	47190	0-2
Gamma	47630	1-4
Delta	48290	3-9
1986U1R	50020	1-2
Epsilon	51140	20-10

(distance is from Uranus' centre to the ring's inner edge)

CHAPTER 16
Neptune

Neptune is the eighth planet from the Sun and the fourth largest (by diameter). Neptune is smaller in diameter but larger in mass than Uranus.

Orbit. 4,504,000,000 km (30.06 AU) from Sun

Diameter: 49,532 km (equatorial)

Mass: 1.0247e26kg

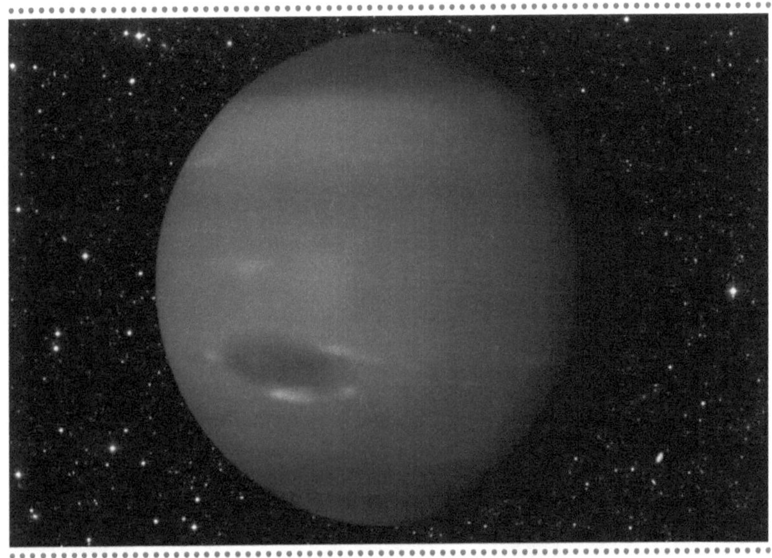

In Roman mythology, Neptune (Greek: Poseidon) was the God of the Sea.

Neptune was first observed by Johann Gottfried on 1846 September 23 very near to the locations independently predicted by Adams and Le Verrier from calculations based on the observed positions of Jupiter, Saturn and Uranus. They are now jointly credited with Neptune's discovery.

Neptune has been visited by only one spacecraft, Voyager 2 on August 25 1989. Much of you know about Neptune comes from this single encounter. But fortunately, recent ground-based and HST observations have added a great deal, too.

Neptune's composition is probably similar to Uranus': Various ices and rocks with about 15% hydrogen and a little helium. There is most likely a small core (about the mass of the Earth) of rocky material Its atmosphere is mostly hydrogen and helium with a small amount of methane.

Neptune's blue colour is largely the result of absorption of red light by methane in the atmosphere but there is some additional as-yet-unidentified chromosphere, which gives the clouds their rich blue tint.

Like Jupiter and Saturn, Neptune has an internal heat source — it radiates more than twice as much energy as it receives from the Sun.

At the time of the Voyager encounter, Neptune's most prominent feature was the Great Dark Spot in the southern hemisphere. It was about half the size as Jupiter's Great Red Spot (about the same diameter as Earth). However, observation; of Neptune in 1994 show that the Great Dark Spot has disappeared. It has either simply dissipated or is currently being masked by other aspects of the atmosphere.

Neptune also has rings. Voyager 2's images showed them to be complete rings with bright clumps. One of the rings appears to have a curious twisted structure. Its names: the outermost is Adams, next is an unnamed ring co-orbital with Galatea, then Leverrier and finally the faint but broad Galle.

Neptune's magnetic field is, like Uranus', oddly oriented and probably generated by motions of conductive material (probably water) in its middle layers.

Neptune has 14 known moons. 7 small named ones and Triton plus four discovered in 2002, one discovered in 2003 and S/2004 N1 in 2013.

Satellite	Distance (000km)	Radius (km)	Mass (kg)
Naiad	48	29	?
Thalassa	50	40	?
Despina	53	74	?
Galatea	62	79	?
Larissa	74	96	?

Proteus	118	209	?
Triton	355	1350	2.14e22
Nereid	5509	170	?
Halimede	15728	61	?
Sao	22422	40	?
Laomedeia	23571	40	?
Psamathe	46695	38	?
Neso	48387	60	?

Neptune's Rings

Ring	Distance (km)	Width (km)
Diffuse	41900	15
Inner	53200	15
Plateau	53200	5800
Main	62930	50

(Distance is from Neptune's centre to the ring's inner edge)

CHAPTER 17
Pluto

Pluto is the farthest planet from the Sun. It is much smaller than any other planet in the solar system and now classified as 'Dwarf Planet' Pluto is smaller than seven of the solar system's moons (the Moon, lo, Europa, Ganymede, Callisto, Titan and Triton).

Orbit: 5,913,520,000 km (39.5 AU) from the Sun (average)

Diameter. 2372 km

Mass: 1.303e22 kg

In Roman mythology, Pluto (Greek: Hades) is the God of the underworld. Pluto was discovered in 1930 by a fortunate accident.

Pluto is the only planet that has not been visited by a spacecraft. Even the Hubble Space Telescope can resolve only the largest features on its surface. On 14 July 2015 the New Horizons spacecraft did a flyby of Pluto after being launched. Pluto has an atmosphere consisting of mainly nitrogen extending to 1,600 km above the surface. Methane is another constituent of the atmosphere and it is likely caused by sunlight breaking down methane gas particles into ethylene and acetylene, which were also discovered by New Horizons. Pluto has five moons: Charon, Hydra, Nix, Kerberos, Styx.

Pluto and Charon size comparisons by New Horizons:

	Diameter	Mass	Density
Pluto	2372 km	1.303e22 kg	1.860 +/- 0.013 g/cm
Charon	1208 km	1.586e21 kg	1.702 +/- 0.021 g/cm

The Pluto-Charon pair orbit about each other around a common center of mass called the barycenter.

Charon was discovered (in 1978 by Jim Christy) just before its orbital plane moved edge-on toward the inner solar system. It was therefore possible to observe many transits of Pluto over Charon and vice versa.

There are some who think Pluto would be better classified as a large asteroid or comet rather than as a planet. Some consider it to be the largest of the Kuiper Belt objects (also known as Trans-Neprjnian Objects).

Pluto's orbit is highly eccentric. At times, it is close to the Sun than to Neptune. Pluto rotates in the opposite direction from most of the other planets.

Like Uranus, the plane of Pluto's equator is at almost right angles to the plane of its orbit.

The surface temperature on Pluto varies between about -235 and -210 C (38 to 63 K), Its density (about 2 gm/cm3) indicates that it is probably a mixture of 70 % rock

and 30 % water ice much like Triton. The bright areas of the surface seem to be covered with ices of nitrogen with smaller amounts of (solid) methane, ethane and carbon monoxide.

Pluto can be seen with an amateur telescope but it is not easy.

Pluto's Satellite Charon

Charon ('KAIR en') is Pluto's only known satellite:

Orbit. 19,500 km from Pluto

Diameter. 1208 km

Mass: 1.586e21kg

Charon is named for the mythological figure who ferried the dead across the River Acheron into Hades (the underworld).

Before Charon was discovered, it was thought that Pluto was much larger since the images of Charon and Pluto were blurred together.

Charon is unusual in that it is the largest moon with respect to its primary planet in the Solar System. Charon's composition is unknown, but its low density (about 2 gm/cm3) indicates that it may be similar to Saturn's icy moons (i.e. Rhea). Its surface seems to be covered with water ice. Interestingly, this is quite different from Pluto.

It has been proposed that Charon was formed by a giant impact similar to the one that formed Earth's Moon. It is doubtful that Charon has a significant atmosphere.

CHAPTER 1 8
The Other Parts of Universe
Black Holes

Imagine an object that is so dense, its gravity so strong that escape velocity is more than 299,792,458 metres per second. That is the speed of light. If Einstein was right and nothing can travel faster than the speed of light, then nothing could reach escape velocity here.

Today's scientists believe that a black hole is the end product in the lifecycle of a giant star. If this star is three or four times as massive as the sun, even after it has exhausted all its fuel, then it can collapse under its own gravity. Just like a crab burying itself at the beach and pulling the sand down over itself, the collapsing star pulls in even-thing around it as well.

Because this dying star has such huge mass, it becomes too strong for even neutrons to resist. It eventually collapses down to one incredibly-dense point, called a singularity. This singularity is surrounded by an event region in which the gravity is so strong that nothing, not even light, can escape.

Anything that crosses a black hole's event, horizon is crushed into an incredibly dense singularity. With the addition of each bit of matter consumed by a black hole, its event horizon continues to expand. The only limit to this expansion is the amount of available matter. It is theoretically possible to consume millions or billions of stars.

In fact, some scientists theorise that rotating black holes (also know as Kerr black holes) which contain billions of dead stars lie at the centres of galaxies.

Black holes are still just a theory, but a very good theory. Now that astronomers have acquired evidence that theoretical white dwarfs and neutron stars really exist, the case for black holes has been strengthened. Since not even light can escape a black hole, then it should be invisible. However, the effects of its massive gravity can be detected.

The idea of black holes was first theorised in the late eighteenth century by English geologist John Mitchell and French astronomer Pierre Simon Laplace. At one time, scientists called them 'gravitationally collapsed objects'. Russian scientists suggested calling them 'collapsars', but it was not until 1969 when Princeton physicist, John Wheeler coined the term black hole. Black holes have continued to hold public interest and are a popular fixture of science fiction books and movies.

CHAPTER 19
Asteroids

Asteroids are material left over from the formation of the solar system. One theory suggests that they are the remains of a planet that was destroyed in a massive collision long ago. More likely, asteroids are material that never coalesced into a planet. In fact, if the estimated total mass of all the asteroids was gathered into a single object, the object would be less than 1,500 kilometres (932 miles) across - less than half the diameter of the Moon.

Thousands of asteroids have been identified from Earth. It is estimated that 100,000 are bright enough to eventually be photographed through Earth based telescopes. Several hundred thousand asteroids have been discovered and given provisional designations so far. Thousands more are discovered each year. There are undoubtedly hundreds of thousands more that are too small to be seen from the Earth. There are 26 known asteroids larger than 200 km in diameter.

Much of the understanding about asteroids comes from examining pieces of space debris that fall to the

surface of Earth. Asteroids that are on a collision course with Earth are called meteoroids. When a meteoroid strikes our atmosphere at high velocity, friction causes this chunk of space matter to incinerate in a streak of light known as a meteor. If the meteoroid does not burn up completely, what is left strikes Earth's surface and is called a meteorite. One of the best places to look for meteorites is the ice cap of Antarctica.

Of all the meteorites examined, 92.8 % are composed of silicate (stone) and 5.7 % are_ composed of iron and nickel. The rest are a mixture of the three materials. Stony meteorites are the hardest to identify since they look very much like terrestrial rocks.

Because of the perturbing influence of the major planets, the asteroid orbits tend to 'wander' and the calculation of whether (or when) a particular object might impact the Earth may require extremely accurate knowledge of the orbit, such as can be provided by radar observations.

The solar system has a large number of rocky and metallic objects that are in orbit around the Sun but are too small to be considered full-fledged planets. These objects are known as asteroids or minor planets. Most, but not all, are found in a band or belt between the orbits of Mars and Jupiter. The Earth is continually encountering interplanetary debris of various sizes. Although the rarity increases with size, you know there are asteroids big enough to cause a catastrophe if they collided with the Earth. Some have orbits that cross Earth's path and there is evidence that Earth has been hit by asteroids in the past.

CHAPTER 20
Comets

A comet is basically a ball of ice and dust that looks like a star with a tail. Some comets do not have tails, looking like hazy, round spots of light.

Most comets have three parts: a nucleus, a head (coma) and a tail.

The 'typical' comet is a small, oblong chunk of ice, about 5-10 miles across, on the average. This chunk of ice is called the comet's 'nucleus'. After the spacecraft Giotto photographed the nucleus of Halley's comet back in 1986, it was learnt that a comet's nucleus probably has a surface that is best described as a black crust. Although the length of the nucleus of Halley's comet is about 12km, it is believed that comet nuclei can range from 1 km to perhaps 50km across. Comet Hale-Bopp of 1997 had a nucleus that was perhaps 40km across.

The black crust of the nucleus helps the comet absorb heat, which in turn causes some of the ices under the crust to turn to a gas. With pressure now building beneath the

crust, the serene, but frozen landscape begins to bulge in places. Eventually, the weakest areas of the crust shatter from the pressure beneath and the gas shoots outward like a geyser and is referred to by astronomers as a jet. Any dust that had been mixed in with the gas is thrown out as well. As more and more jets appear, a tenuous gas and dust shell forms around the nucleus and this is called the coma.

This is a drawing of the region surrounding the nucleus of comet Hale-Bopp on 1997, March 10. This shows an intense emission or jet coming from the nucleus, which is forming features called 'hoods' or arcs within the coma. The hoods are features formed as a result of the rotation of the nucleus. In the case of Hale-Bopp, a new hood was formed nearly every 12 hours.

Comet structures are diverse and very dynamic, but they all develop a surrounding cloud of diffuse material, called a coma that usually grows in size and brightness as the comet approaches the Sun. Usually a small, bright nucleus (less than 10 km in diameter) is visible in the middle of the coma. The coma and the nucleus together constitute the head of the comet.

Many comets are first discovered by amateur astronomers. Since comets are brightest when near the Sun, they are usually visible only at sunrise or sunset.

CHAPTER 21

The Coma and Tail

The Coma

Comets can typically display a coma several thousand kilometres in diameter, with the size being dependent on the comet's distance from the sun and the size of the nucleus. The latter is important because since jets generally spring up on the side of the nucleus facing the sun (that side gets warmest) and since large nuclei have a greater surface area facing the sun, then there is the potential for larger numbers of jets and greater amounts of gas and dust feeding the coma.

One of the largest comets in history was the Great Comet of 1811. It was one of the few comets in history to be discovered with a relatively small telescope at an unusually great distance from the sun, in this case over halfway to the planet Jupiter's orbit. The nucleus has been estimated as between 30 and 40 kilometres in diameter. At one point during September to October 1811, the coma reached a diameter roughly equivalent to the diameter

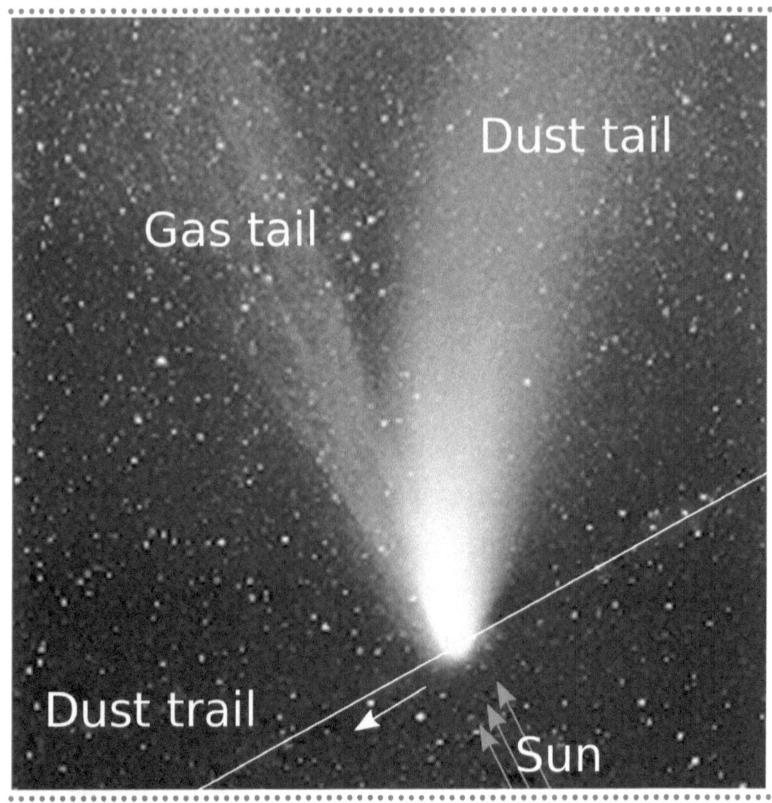

of the sun and was a very notable naked-eye object seen by people around the world. Even though the coma can become quite large, its size can actually decrease about the time it crosses the orbit of Mars. At this distance, the particles streaming out from the sun provide enough force so as to act as a wind and will literally blow the gas and dust particles away from the nucleus and coma. This disruption is the process responsible for a comet's tail, the most spectacular feature of a comet.

The tail

When you have a large comet that moves well inside the orbit of Earth, you have the potential for a long tail. The current record holder for longest tail length is the Great Comet of 1843. Its tail extended more than 250 million kilometres. As the comet comes still closer to the sun, the solar wind — an energetic stream of particles continuously blowing off the sun's surface — encounters the material in the comet's coma and blows it back behind the nucleus. This creates the comet's 'tail', which usually extends behind the comet in the opposite direction from the sun.

You can think of a comet as a large windsock, with the tail extending in the direction of the solar wind's motion. Quite often, two tails will form: one made up primarily of the sublimated gases which have been ionised i.e., electrically charged by the solar wind. It is also called Ion tail and the other one is made up of dust particles. The dust tail is largely insensitive to the Sun's magnetic field and may point in a slightly different direction.

CHAPTER 22
Galaxies

The Milky Way Galaxy is a large disk-shaped system of stars and interstellar matter of which the Sun is a component. It includes the multitude of stars whose light produces the Milky Way, the highly irregular luminous band that encircles the sky. This band of starlight lies roughly in the plane of the galactic disk. This Milky Way system is one of billions of galaxies that make up the universe. It contains several billion stars and large amounts

of dust and interstellar gas and therefore constitutes the most favourable site for new star formation.

The Barred spirals have a nucleus surrounded by a large central bulge with spiral arms coiled around it. These curving arms, which resemble those of a huge pinwheel, are embedded in the galactic disk, which constitutes the main part of the system and measures roughly 70,000 light-years in diameter.

The galactic nucleus is obscured by interstellar dust particles, which absorb both the visible and the ultraviolet light radiated by its components and emissions of radio, infrared, X-ray and gamma ray wavelengths.

These gas clouds are thought to be circling a super-massive object, in all likelihood a black hole with a mass approximately 4,000,000 times that of the Sun. Investigators have determined that the central bulge contains mostly Population II objects (i.e., old stars and star clusters) such as RR Lyrae variable stars and globular clusters.

The components of the spiral arms are quite different. The arms are occupied by objects belonging to the extreme Population I variety (i.e., very young, bright stars and open clusters).

The Sun is located near the inner edge of one of these arms—the Orion arm—about two-thirds of the way from the centre of the Galaxy.

The galactic nucleus lies in the direction of the constellation Sagittarius at a distance of about 27,000 light-years from the Sun.

Above and below the galactic disk is a spherical region (referred to as simply the spherical component) that is occupied by globular clusters and other very old Population II objects—e.g, dwarf stars deficient in the heavy elements.

The entire Milky Way system rotates around the galactic centre, but the various constituent objects do not rotate at the same velocity. Stars distant from the centre travel at lower speeds than do those closer to it.

The Sun, which is located relatively far from the nucleus, moves at an estimated speed of about 225 km per second (140 miles per second) in a nearly circular orbit. Because of its relatively low velocity, the Sun's period of revolution about the galactic centre is approximately 200,000,000 years.

CHAPTER 23
Meteoroids; Meteor Streams and Sporadic Meteors

Meteoroids

Meteoroids are little bits of dust and stone that float around the solar system waiting to strike an atmosphere and burn. Meteors are those bits that hit the Earth's atmosphere and burn away leaving a short fiery tail. Meteorites are those bits of rock, often of asteroid origin, which are large enough to penetrate the atmosphere and hit the Earth's surface. Many tones of meteor dust hit the Earth's atmosphere everyday without ever reaching the ground.

Meteors were originally thought to be part of the atmosphere, like lightening. It has been recorded for millennia that meteors are often seen as a shower. On certain days of the year, many brilliant streaks can be seen every hour.

More than 2000 meteorites have been recovered. They are of different types, Stony meteorites, iron meteorites and

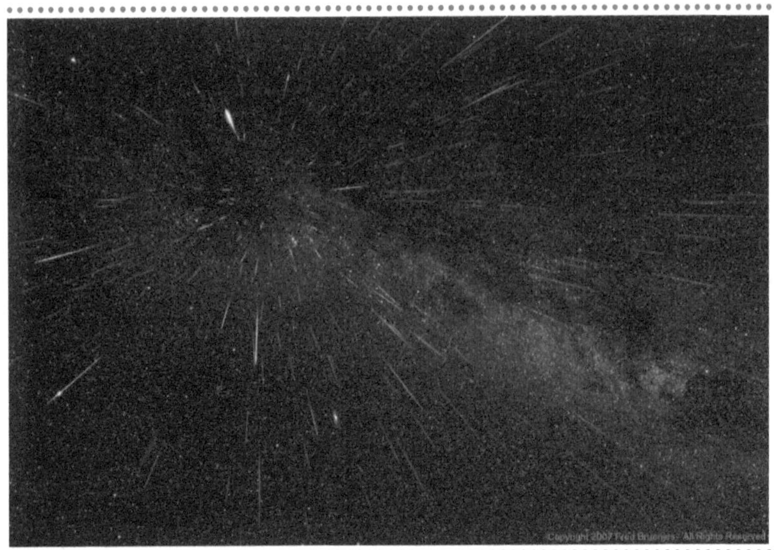

the rare carbonaceous chondrites. The largest meteorite that has been found is the 60 tonne Hoba iron meteorite. The largest stony meteorite weighs about a tonne and the Allende carbonaceous chondrite was a series of chunks that totalled about 5 tonnes.

Impact craters are known on the Earth that corresponds to bodies far larger than these. One of the best known is the Arizona crater in the United States of America, which is 1280 metres across and 180 metres deep. It was formed several thousand years ago by a 250,000 tonne meteorite with a diameter of 70 metres hitting the Earth at a speed of nearly 60,000 km/h.

Meteor streams

Many meteors originated in material stripped off from comets by radiation from the Sun. This material continues to follow the orbit of the originating comet but gets spread out along the orbit. A meteor stream consists of **dust** released from the nucleus of a comet during its **perihelion** passage. Slight differences in the resultant orbital periods cause the individual dust grains to spread out along the orbital path of the parent comet. If the Earth's **orbit** intersects the meteor stream, a **meteor shower** is observed. Many such meteor showers are seen throughout the year. Some are associated with known comets while others are remnants of comets that are unknown. Most showers produce about 20 or so, meteors per hour but there are showers, which can produce thousands of meteors over a period of less than an hour. Such showers are, unfortunately, very rare. Meteor showers are named after the constellation from which they appear to radiate.

Sporadic meteors

Meteors may be seen on any night of the year when the Moon is not bright. If no prominent shower is active then most of the meteors that are seen will come from random directions in space and will thus show no tendency to radiate from any part of the sky. These meteors are called sporadic meteors and about 7 per hour is the normal rate for them to be seen. Most fireballs and meteorites are sporadic meteors. Some rarer types of meteoric matter are believed to have originated on the Moon and on Mars, probably as a result of matter being exploded from the surface by the impact of a large meteorite.

CHAPTER 24
Supernova

Supernova occurs at the end of a star's lifetime, when its nuclear fuel is exhausted and it is no longer supported by the release of nuclear energy. Supernovae are massive giant exploding stars. When the explosion occurs, the resulting illumination can be as bright as an entire galaxy! This will cause a blast wave that ejects the star's envelope into interstellar space. The result of the collapse may be, in some cases, a rapidly rotating neutron star that can be observed many years later as a radio pulsar.

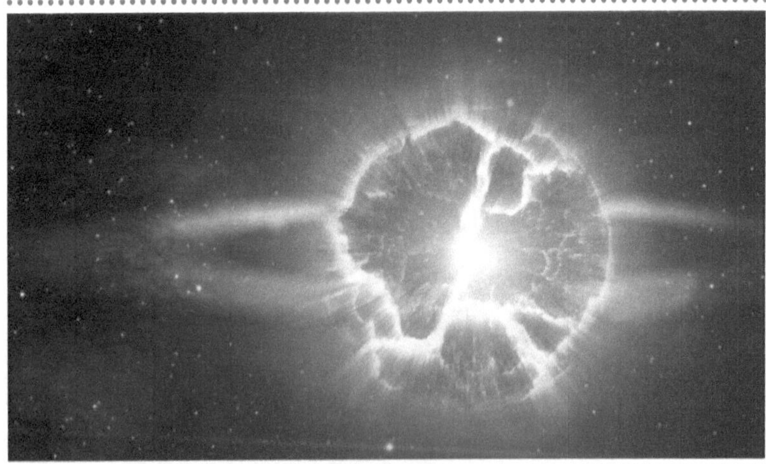

One type of Supernova involves two stars, one of them being a white dwarf whose gravitational attraction is so intense that it is capable of siphoning off material from its companion. Unfortunately for the star (but fortunately for us at a long distance!), the white dwarf exceeds its limit of stability causing it to go into thermonuclear instability and produces one of the largest explosions known in the Universe.

Another type of supernova involves a collapse of the core of a fuel depleted star, tremendous shock waves are generated which cause the outside layers of the star to be blown away from the core. Gravitational forces condensing hydrogen gas raises the temperature at the centre of the star to the point where nuclear fusion is initiated.

Hydrogen is fused into helium and energy is given off in the process. As more helium accumulates at the centre, the temperature rises due to compression until another nuclear fusion is initiated.

A similar process continues with carbon and oxygen fusing to neon, magnesium and oxygen. These elements then undergo another fusion process as the temperature and pressure increase to produce silicon and sulphur. The latter two elements then fuse into iron. During each nuclear fusion, energy is given off.

Since the iron core can collapse only so far and can no longer undergo fusion, it becomes extremely hot and now begins to expand rapidly. This occurs while the star's outer shells are rushing in to fill the void left by the collapsed iron core. The expanding iron and the collapsing outer gases collide with each other producing tremendous shock waves which blow the outer layers away from the core, thus causing the supernova's gigantic explosion.

Actually explosion depends on the type and mass of the progenitor stars, this produce a gas cloud called a supernova remnant which initially expands at a rate of about 10,000 km/s. Gradually, the expansion rate slows down while dissipating into the interstellar medium, seeding the neighbourehood with heavy elements and providing the necessary shock waves for new stellar formation.

Supernovae leave behind a **supernova remnant**, which are often beautiful objects that fade over tens of thousands of years before enriching the interstellar medium with a multitude of chemical elements.

The most famous supernova of recent times is SN1987A. It exploded in the **Large Magellanic Cloud**, was clearly visible to the naked eye, and is one of the best studied objects outside our own **Galaxy**.

www.ingramcontent.com/pod-product-compliance
Lightning Source LLC
LaVergne TN
LVHW051459170726
843492LV00002B/723